# Book Description

The sixties will be forever known as one of the most important and influential periods of all time. A decade that gave us the Space Race, the Beatles, Martin Luther King Jr., the '66 World Cup, Woodstock, and countless other iconic moments, the sixties became a time of almost mythical legend.

Long hair, bright clothes, short skirts, and some of the most incredible music ever recorded brought the youth together in numbers never seen before. It was a time of revolution and technological marvel.

Television was exploding and so was the conflict in Vietnam. Sporting events were being shown worldwide, alongside the horrific news stories that continued to unfold.

The sixties was a time of trying to reunite the people of the world, who had been divided for far too long. It found love and peace battling against hatred and oppression, in a time when the younger generation was finally being heard.

In this book we will take a leisurely stroll through the decade that gave us so many of the ideals we treasure today. Delivered in a conversational tone, it will provide facts and figures in a more smooth and casual way than your regular old history book; because we can't flip through the decade of peace and love without finding our groove, man....

## The 1960s Edition

*Relive the Great Decade That Was the Sixties and Learn Some Facts About Your Childhood Along the Way*

**Paragon Publishing**

## © Copyright 2021 - All rights reserved.

The content contained within this book may not be reproduced, duplicated or transmitted without direct written permission from the author or the publisher.

Under no circumstances will any blame or legal responsibility be held against the publisher, or author, for any damages, reparation, or monetary loss due to the information contained within this book, either directly or indirectly.

Legal Notice:

This book is copyright protected. It is only for personal use. You cannot amend, distribute, sell, use, quote or paraphrase any part, or the content within this book, without the consent of the author or publisher.

Disclaimer Notice:

Please note the information contained within this document is for educational and entertainment purposes only. All effort has been executed to present accurate, up to date, reliable, complete information. No warranties of any kind are declared or implied. Readers acknowledge that the author is not engaged in the rendering of legal, financial, medical or professional advice. The content within this book has been derived from various sources. Please consult a licensed professional before attempting any techniques outlined in this book.

By reading this document, the reader agrees that under no circumstances is the author responsible for any losses, direct or indirect, that are incurred as a result of the use of the information contained within this document, including, but not limited to, errors, omissions, or inaccuracies.

# Table of Contents

Introduction

1960: The Sixties Begin

1961: Winds of Change

1962: Signs of Prosperity

1963: People Remember Exactly Where They Were

1964: Beatlemania

1965: Skirts Get Shorter, Hair Gets Longer

1966: They Think It's All Over...

1967: American Music Fights Back

1968: Assassinations and Vietnam

1969: One Giant Leap For Mankind

References

# Introduction

The sixties was probably the most iconic decade of all time. A generation of freethinkers and musical geniuses were about to play out their lives as the world became enthralled by the Space Race and the conflict in Vietnam. Technological breakthroughs of a magnitude never seen before taught the children of the sixties that anything was possible—even reaching for the stars, which was proven by Neil Armstrong by the end of the decade.

America was in the midst of a racial divide which threatened to split the country in half, as the African Americans finally said, "no more." Assassinations of political figures were becoming the norm; and throughout all the fear, the people continued to try and promote that thing called love.

Music was shifting, and four scamps from Liverpool were preparing to flip the musical world on its head. The landscape was becoming a very different place, and the people who lived there were finally being heard—none more so than the youth.

The sixties was a time of revolution, and the rapid rise of television and broadcasting brought news and information to the masses far more quickly than it ever had before. Women were fighting for equal rights, and as the skirts got shorter and their confidence grew, change swept through the world.

Britain was booming as London became the fashion hub of the world, and the youth were seen donning colorful clothes, long hair, and determined expressions. Europe followed suit, and as income among the people grew for the first time since the Second World War, the Swinging Sixties was free to open itself up to more artistry and culture.

For the first time in decades, the younger generation had no world war to fight, and the population spiked to numbers never seen before. All of this inevitably brought to fruition more creativity, ideas, and opportunities. The sixties was a time of growth, and the achievements and iconic moments it would create would never be equaled.

So, sit back and let the most talked-about decade in history unfold before you. There will be times when it makes you smile, and may even make you feel sad; but one thing it is guaranteed to do is leave you in awe of what the people of the world can achieve when they stand together, hand in hand.

# 1960: The Sixties Begin

Everything changed when the clock struck 12 midnight, and 1959 became the sixties. Not overnight, of course, but even in the first year of the decade everything the Western World thought they knew about society changed. Television was becoming so popular that many homes had one, which had been unthinkable even a few years before. Along with the rise in TV shows came a musical revolution which would forever change the way people viewed their record players.

One of the most important events of 1960 was the beginning of the Space Race. Behind the scenes,

Americans and Soviets had begun to pump millions of dollars into their space programs, in the hope of one day sending man into orbit. It would end up bringing humans much further by the end of the decade, but all of that is for later on.

Ironically, the year that saw the first-ever rise in sales of trousers for women would soon be overtaken by the mini-skirt, which would become a symbol of women's liberation across the globe. Back when a pound or a dollar could buy you a dozen eggs, the newspaper, and a bottle of milk, the ladies of the world were still struggling to have their voices heard.

Rome played host to the Olympics, and the Italians set up many of the events among the backdrop of their historical landmarks. All of this only added to the allure, and the people who watched it live on TV—a first—bore witness to an 18-year-old Muhammad Ali (then Cassius Clay) winning gold as he defeated Zbigniew Pietrzykowski of Poland. Muhammad Ali would again make headlines seven years later when he refused to go to war in Vietnam. The Americans would officially enter the conflict in 1964, sending 3,500 troops overseas to fight for freedom.

The '60 Olympics would see over 5,000 athletes from 83 countries take part. Huge crowds—both at the games and in their living rooms—watched over 150 events take place, with the majority of the medals going home with America, the Soviet Union, and the host, Italy.

In Liverpool, four cheeky chappies were starting to rehearse together in Paul McCartney's parents' front room, unaware that they would soon be mobbed by hormonal teenagers everywhere they went. Their rise to fame would be unprecedented, but in the first year of the decade, the soon-to-be Beatles were just learning their trade.

On both sides of the pond TV was exploding, and in the United States a little show called *The Flintstones* was all the rage. As Americans were being introduced to Fred and the gang in Bedrock, their more serious neighbors in Britain had just been introduced to Ken Barlow and the people of Weatherfield, in the hit TV soap opera *Coronation Street*. In this year alone, 100 million televisions were being used worldwide.

In the year that saw Joanne Woodward become the first star on the Hollywood Walk of Fame, movie-goers were privileged to be part of cinematic history. Blockbusters drew people to the felt-covered seats of their local theaters like never before, and hits such as *Spartacus, Psycho,* and *Swiss Family Robinson* paved the way for a new dawn in cinema.

At the Brighton Toy Fair, imported toys were finally being showcased, and word on the street was that France's latest craze, the Loopy Loop, was destined to do the same in America and Britain as it had in the rest of Europe. It did no such thing, however, and the simplistic but highly entertaining Lego was the toy that all of the kids demanded that Christmas.

D.H. Lawrence's novel *Lady Chatterley's Lover* was finally published commercially after 32 years of being banned. As tame as the words might seem today, they were considered obscene in 1928. Although such a victory may seem insignificant for publishers like Penguin, it was a massive step toward creative freedom.

America was having its own literary breakthrough, as Harper Lee's *To Kill a Mockingbird* was also published to universal acclaim. A book that pointed to the racial inequality that was still raging in the States was bound to ruffle feathers, and it did. Even when it won the

Pulitzer Prize, many people cried out for it to be taken off the shelves.

Though the Flower Power movement had not begun just yet, younger people started protesting on school and college grounds in Britain and the United States, respectively. The Ban the Bomb rally took place in London in April; and in America, people were starting to show signs of unrest at their entering the Vietnam War.

John F. Kennedy and Richard Nixon took part in the first-ever televised presidential debate in Chicago. Nixon, who looked wound up and shaky throughout, would go on to be thoroughly outshone by his younger and more handsome opponent. Kennedy would become the darling of American politics, but his reign would be tragically cut short.

Licorice and toffee were still the sweets of choice in most of Europe, while the Americans, who had access to ample sugar at much lower cost, had moved on to Pixie Sticks and Starburst. Long before censored advertising, these sugar-filled treats were promoted without restraint.

This amazing year saw the invention of both the laser and the pacemaker, while Xerox released their first commercial photocopier. Hugh Hefner opened the first of his Playboy Clubs in Chicago, further freeing the younger generation from the shackles of old. All of this was done to the sound of Chubby Checker telling kids to do the Twist, and the album *Elvis is Back* was released.

An air of change was descending, especially upon the Western World. The youth were finding their voice, and new ideas were starting to form. Technology was advancing at a rate never seen before, and it all seemed to coincide with the belief that anything was possible. In a nutshell, 1960 was the beginning of freedom- intellectual, sexual, and artistic. It had its dark moments too, but all in all, most people who lived through it would look back with affection.

# 1961: Winds of Change

Although the Space Race would soon grip the world—especially America—in '61, the most popular TV shows were *Wagon Train*, *Gunsmoke*, and *Bonanza*. Toy guns, holsters, and plastic Sheriff badges were the order of the day for young boys, while a slim-waisted, long-legged doll named Barbie was becoming all the rage for the girls. The Slip 'n Slide was causing injuries in most back gardens, and Lego still reigned supreme worldwide.

In politics, only one story really mattered. A certain John Fitzgerald Kennedy became the 35th President of the United States of America in January. His few short years as the most powerful man in the world would be consumed chiefly by sending men into space and trying to defuse the Cold War, which had held a constant fear over the world for decades. It would continue to do so for many more years, but the intensity would fade after a while.

Kennedy's charm and good looks, combined with his masterstroke of playing on his Irish-Catholic roots, would help him win the election. Many Americans at the time were, in fact, Irish-Americans, having fled there during the famine in their homeland. To have someone they related to running for president seemed like a dream come true, and it gained him millions of guaranteed votes.

In the rapidly escalating Space Race, the Soviets took a mammoth-sized step ahead of their American enemies when cosmonaut Juri Gargarin became the first man in history to orbit Earth. Alan Shepard had made it to space a few months earlier, but only for 15 minutes. The American people, still reveling in the celebrations of electing the man who would bring "hope, peace, and freedom to every American," were shocked that another nation could outdo them, especially in something so technologically advanced.

In Europe, the construction of the first phase of the Berlin Wall was completed. The barrier cruelly separated German family, friends, and colleagues until it was finally torn down in 1989. West Germany would thrive far better during this period than their eastern neighbors, both economically and socially; and it would take another year after the last bit of brick had fallen for the country to be called simply Germany again.

Meanwhile, in Morges, Switzerland, the offices of the WWF (not the wrestling franchise!) were being set up after the combined efforts of Victor Stolan, Sir Julian Huxley, and Edward Marx Nicholson. Under the original name of the World Wildlife Fund, they would go on to save millions of endangered and mistreated animals the world over. Through their fundraising efforts, the organization is bigger now than ever.

Westerns and dramas were big hits in theaters. The latter became more popular with each passing year, as people now wanted to be intellectually entertained as they chomped down on their popcorn. A little cartoon called *101 Dalmatians* blew them all out of the water though, and the Disney hit would go on to gross over $102 million, with inflation taken into account.

On the UK singles chart, Elvis Presley, The Everly Brothers, and Helen Shapiro still filled the shelves of the music stores, hinting that rhythm and blues and gospel was still in demand. It would be another couple of years before the Beatles would change all of that, opening the door for the British Invasion not only to consume Europe, but America too. Their influence would pave the way for an array of talented bands and musicians to fill the charts as the decade progressed.

Elvis, Patsy Cline, and Roy Orbison were still popular in America, suggesting that cleaner, country ballads were what the people wanted. Unbeknownst to the parents of every young teenager in the States, four kids with floppy hair were soon going to change all of that; but in '61, they were only setting up their equipment in the Cavern Club in Liverpool.

Regardless of the feel-good factor of Kennedy's election, America fell into a 10-month recession between April of 1961 and February of '62. Unemployment grew by a massive 7%, mainly due to the rise in conveyor belt production. Thousands of people in automobile construction and many other businesses continued to be replaced by rotors and presses. Henry Ford had passed on years before, but Fordism was thriving more than ever.

Harper Lee, who had won the Pulitzer Prize the previous year for *To Kill a Mockingbird*, went one step further in '61 by taking home the Nobel Prize for Literature. *The Apartment* cleaned up at the Oscars, and Mickey Mantle became the seventh Major League Baseball player to make 400 runs. While in Britain, the Spurs became the first club in English footballing history to win the double. At Wimbledon, Angela Mortimor from England won the Women's Singles title. Rod Laver, an Australian, lifted the men's.

A failed landing operation on the Bay of Pigs, funded by the American government, led to further strain on the relations between Cuba, the United States, and the Soviet Union. Operation Zapata would be one of John

F. Kenney's first significant decisions as president; and the failure, along with the recent recession, caused him severe issues early on in his tenure.

The Suicide Act of 1961 was introduced in England, as people became aware that mental struggles are not a sign of weakness but something that needs to be treated. The world would have a long way to go to get to where it needed to be, but the first step had been taken.

All of this would come a little too late for Ernest Hemmingway. The author of such masterpieces as *For Whom the Bell Tolls* and *The Sun Also Rises* killed himself with his favorite shotgun at his home in Idaho. The Nobel Prize winner had struggled with alcoholism through most of his adult life, and coupled with his onset of mental illness, decided to cut his life short.

Although 1960 had opened the door for intellectual and artistic freedom, '61 seemed determined to try and slam it shut again. Despite all of the struggles and threats of more war, the good intentions of '60 continued to push on. Music, TV, literature, and ideals were changing, and the people of the world were starting to wake up to passions and creativity that they had never known could be theirs.

The year of '61 can probably be seen as the birth of the younger generation. Both world wars were now firmly in the past, and the youth outnumbered the older generation for the first time in decades. Although the Cold War meant that most people kept one eye on the sky, the younger generation stayed home and blossomed instead of being sent off to fight for their country at 18. This was bringing different perspectives into the world that would go on to shape the rest of the decade, and on until the present.

# 1962: Signs of Prosperity

Throughout the Western World, the Teddy Boy look still had the young men wearing tight jeans and grease in their hair. Cliff Richard was crooning his way to the top of the British charts, while Acker Bilk and Ray Charles were hits in the good ol' US of A. People there were also going crazy for a little dance called The Mashed Potato, proving that the Americans were in desperate need of some real music to sail across the Atlantic and save them from the generic, sugary pop of old.

The Beach Boys had just released their first album, *Surfin' Safari*, and the title track would spawn the California sound. Young people were now wearing shorter shorts and bikinis, although this sort of freedom among the youth would be confined to the western states for now, as the craze was only in the process of sweeping along the coast.

JFK had found his feet in his presidential role, and by February the mini-recession that had threatened to drag America back into the Depression of the '30s had ended. With the Cold War having caused fear throughout the globe for decades, Kennedy tried everything in his power to put an end to the Cuban Missile Crisis. Those five weeks in the winter of '62 had seen the children of the world hiding under their school desks in precaution for the nuclear fallout that seemed inevitable.

The American president had held an emergency meeting with nine members of the National Security Council (NSC) to try and extinguish the flames that had threatened to get out of control after the Bay of Pigs. That failed attempt at disrupting Cuban/Soviet relations had prompted the Soviets to place nuclear missiles on Cuban soil in an effort to prevent future American invasions. Kennedy, who had been instructed to threaten the NSC with more severe violence if his demands weren't met, went against his advisors and decided on a more diplomatic approach. A fragile but important agreement was hammered out, stating that the United States was to refrain from invading Cuba if the Soviets would dismantle their bombs and return them to Soviet soil.

In Britain, Harold MacMillan was starting to bring new prosperity to the people, and the first real upturn in fortunes and profits since the war was beginning to make people believe again. Rations were now a thing of the past, and the younger generation was finally starting to have a voice. New ideas and prospering businesses were the order of the day, and things that had never mattered before, such as fashion and art, were starting to take center stage among the younger adults.

The Beatles had just released their first single, "Love Me Do," but it would only chart at number 47. It seemed that the Liverpudlians would have to wait just a little bit longer before they conquered the world. The average house price in Britain was £2,614, and a pint of milk would only set you back four pence. Drinking a pint of bitter was a little steeper, at 11 p, and a copy of the newspaper was just a little over one penny.

Across the pond, a new abode would come in at around $12,000, while a gallon of milk was a buck. Average rent was $100 a month, but an education at Harvard University would set you back roughly $1,500. Compared to today's prices for a top education in the States—even with inflation taken into account—that is a hell of a lot cheaper.

Kids' toys had started to change too. Plastic cap guns and other similar toys had given way to space-themed creations, such as the Moon Landing Set. Etch-a-Sketch was seen as the fanciest of toys, while the massive popularity of *The Flintstones* television series in America had seen huge sales in the Flintstones Building set. Other popular toys included Chatty Cathy dolls, Flintstones Pedal Car, Tammy Doll outfits, and Mr. Mercury.

In sports, the '62 World Cup took place in Santiago, Chile, with the mighty Brazil becoming only the second team in history to retain the trophy when they beat Czechoslovakia by two goals in the final. The whole tournament was marred by violence on the pitch, as many games became nothing but a field for 22 men to kick lumps out of each other. The worst such occurrence was at the Battle of Santiago, in a match that would see the host and Italy go head-to-head, with both sets of players seemingly forgetting that there was a ball involved. BBC commentator David Coleman went on to describe it as "the most stupid, appalling, disgusting, and disgraceful exhibition of football, probably in the history of the game" (Coleman, 1962).

Sam Walton would open the first-ever Walmart in Arkansas in '62, leading the way for commercialism and consumerism to become all about quantity over quality. An attitude of "why buy a small block of artisan cheese for five bucks, when you can bury yourself in a family bag of Cheetos for a dollar" seemed to sweep the nation quite quickly, and has remained, in some shape or form, ever since.

In August, the darling of Hollywood, Marilyn Monroe, died of suspected suicide at her home in Los Angeles. Her psychiatrist discovered her body after being called to the house by Miss Monroe's housekeeper, who had suspected something wasn't right. The death sent shockwaves through the world, which, despite the Suicide Act of the previous year, was still very uneducated in the severity of mental health issues. Given Monroe's almost unrestricted access to heavy prescription medication, it had been very easy for her to overdose and had probably only been a matter of time.

In the ever more competitive Space Race, the Americans were still playing catch up. John Glenn achieved what Yuri Gargarian had done the year before for the Soviets when he successfully orbited the Earth. All of this coincided with JFK making the bold claim that the Americans would have a man on the Moon by the end of the decade. To most, if not everyone, this target seemed unattainable; and the majority of people believed it to be nothing more than "big talk" from a man who knew that the Soviets were much further ahead.

The iconic superhero Spiderman first appeared in a comic when he made a small cameo in Amazing Fantasy number 15. DC and Marvel had now become rival distributors. Their competitiveness would spawn multi-billion-dollar franchises as the younger generation began to crave more graphic and hardcore entertainment in the comics they read.

With the sixties still in their infancy, the changes that would go on to shape the world were just beginning to find their feet. Much of this was down to the continuing explosion of television, and the cost of owning a TV becoming a lot more attainable to the average household. Soon, endless amounts of news, music, and entertainment were being beamed into the majority of homes, and kids were suddenly seeing the world as they never had before.

Now, the average little boy or girl could look up to someone who made a living out of doing the things they did for fun; and to top it off, the people on the screen were wearing flamboyant clothes, singing rock 'n' roll, and dancing unashamedly. The constant fear being broadcast on the news ignited a revolution in the teenagers' blood, and they started to find a voice that said, "No, we won't stand for this."

Gone were the days of Mommy and Daddy knowing best, and this cubic portal into the world opened their eyes at a much younger age as to how life really worked. Revolution was creeping into the music being played in the pubs and clubs around the world, and the teenagers who came together there were hearing things that nobody had ever told them before.

These songs, and the words they carried, would creep into the charts in years to come; but for now, the rumbling of discontent in the younger generation was still only simmering at the surface. It would soon boil over, and what poured out was color, musical expression, and revolt.

# 1963: People Remember Exactly Where They Were

After only a couple of years as the President of the United States of America, John F. Kennedy was assassinated on Friday, November 22, 1963. In a world before seemingly weekly mass shootings in the States, this murder sent shockwaves like never before through the world as a whole. Everyone would have a story to tell from that day forward, and it usually began with, "I remember exactly where I was when..."

Kennedy had been riding in a motorcade through Dealey Plaza with his wife, Jacqueline, when Lee Harvey Oswald shot him. Medics tried their best to revive the president, but Oswald—who would be arrested 70 minutes later—was a trained ex-Marine, and his shot had proven fatal. The killer would be murdered himself as he left the Dallas Police Department by Jack Ruby as the nation watched on live TV. These events would lead to an array of conspiracy theories that still rage today.

Earlier in the year, things had been looking up for the country. Among the seething tensions surrounding racial inequality, Martin Luther King Jr gave his famous "I have a dream" speech to 250,000 supporters at the Lincoln Memorial in Washington DC. MLK, who had peacefully fought for the rights of African

Americans for years, spoke so well and with such unadulterated passion that he roused something not only in the people who were in attendance, but in the millions who have heard it since then.

In Britain, the Beatles had their first number one hit when "From Me to You" stormed the charts and set in motion the British Invasion period that was about to set sail for America. They would follow this with a number one album, as *Please Please Me* sold at an unprecedented rate. The younger people finally heard the music they desired on the airwaves, which had never happened before.

A lot of this had to do with a rise in pirate radio stations like Radio Caroline and Radio London, which were transmitting from anchored boats and unused sea forts. Because they rested in international waters, the authorities couldn't do much about it. The allure of listening to something that would otherwise have been deemed illegal spoke to the kids even more. As we've seen in the few previous years of the sixties, a revolution was indeed in the air.

In entertainment, Doctor Who premiered on British TV, spawning a franchise that would keep running until the present day. That year, the hit movies included *Cleopatra, The Birds, Dr. No,* and *How the West Was Won*. Along with all of the arts, cinema was shifting to a more intellectual curve, a trend that would spike in the years that followed as psychedelic drugs and new, groovy ideas swamped the entertainment business.

This year also saw Kim Philby named as "The Third Man" in the British spy ring that had defected to the Soviet Union. Much of the information they had procured and passed onto the Soviets would cost the British millions in repairing the damage, and the new public enemy number one would escape to Moscow, where he would live out the rest of his days in hiding.

In sport, Jack Nicklaus won his first Masters golf tournament, while Arnold Palmer became golf's all-time leading moneymaker. The Chicago Bears lifted the National Football League trophy, beating the New York Giants. Spurs became the first British club to win a European trophy when they claimed the Cup Winners Cup, and Everton won the English Football League.

In Britain, The Great Train Robbery took place as a gang of 15, led by Bruce Reynolds, stole 2.4 million pounds from a Royal Mail train traveling from Glasgow to London. Most of the gang would later be arrested, but a few were never apprehended. Much of the money stolen (which would amount to over $50 million today) was never found. Ronnie Biggs, one of the men arrested, would later escape from jail and live out the rest of his days in exile, making him a celebrity who would go on to sell books and movie rights in the following years.

In the Space Race, the Soviets sent Valentina Tereshkova into orbit, further damaging the reputation of America. In a time when women's rights were still being fought for, this was seen as an attempted slap in the face of the Americans, who had remained one step behind their Soviet enemies the whole way through. With the death of JFK, the people of America began to fear the worst once more, as their bubble of invincibility as a nation seemed to be constantly getting poked at by their enemies.

Although it would only be a couple of years until Mary Quant shocked Britain—and the rest of the Western World—with the mini-skirt, knee-high hems were still the order of the day for the ladies. Excess makeup was seen as unclassy, and more natural hairstyles were in fashion. The Teddy Boy look was being replaced by longer, 'Beatle' haircuts and smart suits for the men. Switching the style of the Liverpudlian rockers had come from the creative mind of Brian Epstein, their manager, and the cute, respectable look would go a long way in helping them crack America in the following years.

People were also given the news that the first-ever liver transplant had taken place. When Dr. Michael DeBakey pioneered an artificial heart that could be used during heart transplant procedures, it caused many people to fear that science was going too far. A lot of this kind of news, along with the world's almost feverish obsession with space, would help the Sci-Fi genre, both in movies and books, to explode.

Even after the death of Marilyn Monroe the year before, the sedative Valium was mass-produced and made available to millions. Although it was advertised as an aid for depression and anxiety, the lenient policing on who it could be prescribed to and how addictive it could be would go on to cause more damage than it fixed.

The audio cassette was introduced, allowing teenagers to record the songs they loved off of the radio. In LA, the iconic music venue The Whisky A-Go-Go opened its doors, proving that a need for deeper, more meaningful music was spreading. The younger people needed somewhere to go where the artists they idolized could be themselves and give them the music they desired.

Even with the death of a wonderful president, Martin Luther King Jr and Malcolm X's emergence showed that America, along with the rest of the world, was ready for change. In '63, things seemed to be moving at light speed, and all of this playing out against the backdrop of the Space Race and the mind blowing advances in medicine sent chills of fear through the older generation, who felt that things were moving too fast.

For the younger people, speaking and being heard was something entirely new, and the air was filled with a sort of explosive tension as generations' worth of things that needed to be said were about to come out all at once. Most of the changes that would result from this would be positive, but as we have seen repeatedly through history, every positive action brings an equally negative reaction.

# 1964: Beatlemania

With the continuing explosion of popular music among the youth, the BBC saw an opportunity and first aired the chart show, *Top of the Pops*. Now the people of Britain could see what was hot in the music world. Live performances and a rundown of the top 40 hits each week gave them another window, right next to pirate radio, to view the bands and artists that were ripping up the rule book. The same television company would also first air the now-iconic *Match of the Day*, bringing all of the afternoon's scores and highlights to the football fans of Britain in one tidy package.

Along with this musical breakthrough, the £10 note was rereleased into circulation—something that had not happened since the Second World War, further proving that Britain was on the rise. Harold Wilson had been elected Prime Minister, making him the youngest man in history to do so. Wilson's securing this position at such a young age (politically speaking) was further proof that the young people were now being listened to. There was a feel-good factor spreading through the streets, and London was on the verge of becoming the trendiest city in the world. With the high spirits came opportunity, and a wave of new fashion outlets and record stores sprang up all over the country.

On February 9, the Beatles made their historic appearance on the Ed Sullivan show to a chorus of deafening screams. Beatlemania was heating up, and several teenage girls had to be hospitalized through fainting at the sheer sight of the mop-topped quartet. Staggeringly, two months later, the band held all top five spots on the American charts—something that would be unthinkable today.

China, which had remained surprisingly quiet throughout the nuclear standoff that worried the world, exploded their first atomic weapon on a test site, further raising tensions that war was always just a red button away. Along with Britain, France, America, and the Soviet Union, they became the fifth nation to have access to nuclear weapons, though they promised that they would not be the first to use them.

Dr. Martin Luther King received the Nobel Prize in Oslo, becoming only the second African American to receive such an honor. It would also make him the youngest recipient of the prize to that date, further showing the massive leaps in social equality that one man could make if he were true to his cause.

At the Convention Hall in Miami Beach, a 22-year-old Cassius Clay (soon to be Muhammad Ali) defeated the heavy favorite, and much feared, Sonny Liston in a seventh-round technical knockout. Liston, who had twice destroyed previous champion Floyd Patterson, was expected to do the same to the cocky kid from Louisville. But Clay shocked the world with his fleet-footed precision and takedown of the champ.

Two days after he became Champion of the World, Cassius Clay attended a party in Miami with his good friend, Malcolm X. In the months the followed, the young man would become enthralled by The Nation of Islam and their belief that the African Americans deserved better than what they had. In a couple of days, Cassius had become a member, and later that year, he would denounce the name 'Clay,' given its roots in slavery, and declare that he would be known as Muhammad Ali from that day forward.

Lyndon Johnson, who had taken the presidential hot seat following the assassination of John F. Kennedy, stepped up America's involvement in the Vietnam War—something that would heavily divide opinion across the globe. The youth of America, who were being sent off to fight for a cause they barely understood, felt inspired by the music and expressionist views around them, and they took to the streets in protest. Along with the Race Riots breaking out across the States, the previously positive feeling of cultural revolution was starting to look more like the traits attributed to the beginnings of civil war.

Sidney Poitier won the Best Actor Award at the Oscars, becoming the first African American to do so. The movies catching the world's attention were *Mary Poppins*, *My Fair Lady*, and *Goldfinger*. The profit margin in creating a blockbuster hit was becoming astronomical, and the movie business was now one of the most profitable and glamorous things to be associated with. America's obsession with all things Hollywood would lead to a less healthy one, where celebrity in any form was to be considered essential, regardless of how it was achieved.

America had launched the uncrewed Mariner in November, with its mission to beam back the first-ever photographs of Mars. It would succeed in this the following year, and the first images of the Red Planet would be snapped at a distance of just over 10,000 miles. As impressive as this was, it wasn't seen as important to the American public as getting a man on the Moon, which had, of course, been promised by JFK the previous year. The people wanted to know where their half a billion dollars in taxes on the Space Program had gone.

IBM introduced the System/360 at the New York World's Fair. The computer, about the size of a Portapotty, was still far too expensive to be sold to the general public, but many of the larger businesses of the world began to use them. It was a scientific breakthrough of such magnitude that the history of the planet would be changed forever. Of course, although impressed, the people in attendance at the World's Fair could not have been aware of just how important the machine they were viewing would become.

Ford released a handful of the new model, the Mustang, in mid '64, starting a craze for smaller, more sleek, and sportier cars. When Tania Mallet drove the 1964 Mustang Convertible in the movie *Goldfinger*, this need to have a car that could compete with Bond's signature Aston Martin only grew among the public.

In the summer of '64, the 15th Olympic Games took place in Tokyo, Japan. Keeping with the technological breakthroughs of recent years, it was the first Olympics to use computers to mark scores and times in certain events. Japan also used the Games to showcase how quickly they had rebuilt after the war and prove to the rest of the world that they were now a peaceful nation, only concerned with economic and social growth.

The United States and the Soviet Union would battle to be crowned the outright winner, with America winning more gold but the Soviets bringing home more total medals. Japan would come a distant third, but the main focus was on how superbly the Games had been organized. Japan had proved that they were a nation of hardworking, dedicated people who had clearly managed to flourish after the devastation of years past.

After the artistic and musical changes of the previous years, '64 appeared to veer toward the technological side of things once more. Although the Beatles had smashed all records in the States and Europe by dominating the charts, their near monopolization of the airwaves momentarily pushed any other bands aside. This gave other artists something to aim for, of course, and the wave of new music that came around over the next decade and a half would forever remain unparalleled, both in quality and in its message.

Amidst the unrest in America, there was also hope. Businesses were beginning to prosper again. The boom in affordable electronics such as TVs, record players, electric shavers, and many other gadgets gave the country a futuristic feel. Sweet (or candy) wrappers were even becoming more colorful, and brands like Coca-Cola could clog the magazines and television ads with impunity. Children from around the world looked on in envy as America was portrayed as a magical place full of wonder.

Europe saw a renaissance of its own, and much like America, the younger people were having a lot more of an impact. Fortunes could now be made out of cunning, perseverance, and opportunity; where before, only the elite, expensively-educated had these doors opened to them. An "if you want something, go and get it" attitude was spreading, and one word that might best describe 1964 is 'hope.'

# 1965: Skirts Get Shorter, Hair Gets Longer

Aleksei Leonov became the first man to walk in space when he exited the Voskhod space capsule, attached to a 16-foot tether, for over 12 minutes. It was another huge step—or giant leap—for the Soviets in the Space Race, and it added immense pressure on the Americans to step up their game. The public had spent a lot of tax dollars on the Space Program, and they were yet to see any results that the Soviets had not already achieved.

Like their American cousin, Britain was in the midst of racial tensions. Although they had fewer immigrants, they were long-established, and as British as anyone else. The discrimination faced was horrific, and the *1965 Race Relations Act* was brought in to try and educate people on such matters. It would take another decade for this to really take hold; and even with the new legislation, small shops and boarding houses were excluded, so they were still allowed to deny people entry based on the color of their skin.

The English public was starting to think about the World Cup, as the summer of the following year would see the greatest event in sports being played out in stadiums around the country. Preparations were already in place, and the people of England demanded success in a competition that, up until '62, the English

Football Association had tried to dismiss as beneath them. Even after Hungary's demolition of England at Wembley more than a decade before, the English had been too stubborn to admit that football had moved on without them. This would be their chance to reclaim it.

Mary Quant, one of the torch-bearers of the Swinging Sixties, would release the mini-skirt to national and global success—and outrage, in equal measure. Women were starting to wear what they wanted, and not what society dictated. Quant, who would also take credit for 'hot-pants,' became a celebrity in her homeland, and her fashion articles and new ideas were anticipated like the release of a new song or movie.

London was becoming a hotbed for expression, and it seemed that all of the arts were mixing and becoming one. Now the kids could see the people they idolized wearing different styles and fashions on the TV in their front room, and they could take inspiration from these pop stars and actors. Being artistic was now more credible and not something to be ashamed of, while freedom to be who you wanted to be was becoming much more acceptable.

In February of '65, Malcolm X was assassinated by the Nation of Islam as he prepared to give a speech at Audubon Ballroom in Manhattan. He had expressed in an interview the previous year his fears that such a thing would happen; yet, he'd continued to give his talks on racial inequality. Unlike his peer, Martin Luther King Jr, Malcolm didn't believe in the peaceful protest approach. He didn't promote violence, but he was adamant that the African American people had to defend themselves by any means possible. His funeral was attended by 30,000 followers, all of whom mourned the loss of an outstanding advocate for human rights.

A month after the death of Malcolm X, MLK Jr and his followers completed a five-day, 54-mile peaceful march from Selma, Alabama to the steps of Montgomery, where he addressed a massive crowd that had already been endlessly campaigning for equal voting rights. He told them that they were bearing witness to a monumental moment in history, and that their non-violent approach bore more fruit than aggressive tactics. Given that Malcolm X's murder was still fresh in their minds, understandably making them angry, it only goes to prove his talents as a public speaker that he was able to keep tensions from simmering over.

At this time, the conflict in Vietnam was escalating, and the younger generation who had not been forced to fight yet were beginning to protest more regularly. On the other side, a large majority of this generation still felt a need to fight for their country regardless of the reasoning behind it, and they signed up for military service in droves. The split in everyone's perspective on the war would slam a divide between them, which the government would use to their advantage.

After their historic appearance on the Ed Sullivan Show—and subsequent domination of the music charts—the Beatles created the term "stadium rock" when they played to over 55,000 fans at Shea Stadium. It was the first date of their American tour, and the band could be seen looking out over the crowd in disbelief. Throughout the performance, John, Paul, George, and Ringo were unable to hear their instruments through the fervent screams of the teenagers in attendance. The 2,000 strong security had their work cut out for them, as several audience members collapsed and fainted.

G.I. Joe was one of the biggest selling toys that year, proving that only a small majority was protesting Vietnam so far. Toy soldiers and tanks would fly off the shelves as the kids tried to imitate the action they saw on the news channels. Fisher-Price released their almost indestructible Chatter Phone, a toy that was built so well that they can still be found perfectly intact in the attics and basements of homes today. Pedal cars, the electric organ, and even a Honda pedal bike were popular for the more well-off kids.

Barbie had pretty much monopolized the girls' market, and the introduction of her little sister, Skipper, tightened the toy's stranglehold even more. This not only gave Mattel another angle by which to hock Barbie dolls, but it also meant that they could basically double production of the same sets of clothes to coincide with the "dress them in matching outfits" marketing approach. Also out that year was the Tressy Doll, where the little ones could grow or shorten their doll's hair as fashion dictated.

In sports, Liverpool won the English F.A. Cup, defeating Leeds United in the final. Golf saw Jack Nicklaus top the earnings once more, and the Green

Bay Packers lifted the National Football League. The Dodgers took the World Series, and Arkle romped home in the Cheltenham Gold Cup.

In the much-anticipated rematch between Sonny Liston and Muhammad Ali, two major events in boxing history would occur. All of this was made more staggering by the fact that the fight only lasted half a round. In the space of a few seconds, boxing would shoot into a stratosphere never seen before, as Ali landed the now-famous "phantom punch." It was so labeled because the 2,500 people in attendance claimed that they never saw the hit landing. Luckily, the fight was broadcast on television, and experts have since proven that the punch was genuine—and not, in fact, Liston taking a fall, as many had claimed.

The image of Ali standing over his fallen foe and shouting down into his face is one of the most iconic pictures in sporting history, and would go on to adorn the walls of millions of students' bedrooms and man caves to this day. Liston, who had refused to refer to Ali by his new name in the lead-up to the fight, had clearly enraged his opponent, and the photograph seems to catch all of this pent-up aggression coming out in a split second.

Beatlemania was still picking up speed in America and the rest of the world, but '65 was a year of tension as well as love. The voice of a generation was straining to be heard over the gunfire in Vietnam, and the public's growing need for information was leading to the fall of many celebrities and public figures. Their dirty laundry seemed to be pasted to the front page of every newspaper around the globe each morning.

The death of Malcolm X proved that America had a long way to go yet, but the cultural revolution that had begun in London and spread through Europe was starting to reach the States. Peace and love was a fantastic concept, and in a time of conflict and tension, it would be a much-needed tonic for the masses. Almost like a bookmark, '65 was a year that seemed to represent the halfway point in a decade that had been trying to make up its mind about which direction it wanted to go.

# 1966: They Think It's All Over...

In the Space Race, the Soviets landed the uncrewed Luna 9 on the Moon, making them the first nation in history to land an object on a celestial body successfully. With all of these advances in space travel catching the world's attention, television jumped on the bandwagon; and TV shows *Star Trek* and *Lost in Space* aired their first episodes to worldwide acclaim and wonder. Sci-Fi was reopening a door for a whole new creative outlet that had been shut since the first boom of the genre in the twenties, with sales of comics and science fiction-based books flying off the shelves.

The American population hit its highest number ever at over 195 million people, but Lyndon Johnson and his advisors were doing everything in their power to keep that number down. By '66, they had sent half a million soldiers to Vietnam to fight for their cause, with many coming home in body bags. Numbers like this fanned the flames of already wild tension, and much of the younger generation dug their heels in and refused to go.

College kids burned their draft papers in protest, and Muhammad Ali publicly refused to fight a war that had nothing to do with him. He would be stripped of the heavyweight title he had worked so hard to get, but his actions would inspire many African Americans to say 'no' to fighting for a country that barely saw them as citizens back then.

Ali had already amassed a staggering five fights in '66 alone, a number that would be unthinkable today in boxing, where most fighters rarely have more than one. In other sports, Liverpool won the English First Division, while their neighborhood rivals, Everton, claimed the prestigious F.A. Cup. Real Madrid, who had won the first five European Cups in a row, lifted the trophy again in '66, ending a five-year wait.

The biggest sporting event that year happened at Wembley Stadium, when England defeated their bitter rivals West Germany 4-2 in a match that would forever go down in history for three timeless moments. The first of these was the heated debate over whether Geoff Hurst's effort had crossed the line or not. Before the advances in goal-line technology that we have today, Tofiq Bahramov's eagle-eyed, split-second decision would make him forever known as "The Russian Linesman."

Bahramov's decision to award a goal that would be part of Geoff Hurst's historic hat trick would be debated for decades, but thankfully for Englishmen all over the world, recent technology has proven that The Russian Linesman had been correct. Hurst's hat trick would be the only time that one player scored three goals in a World Cup final, a record that still stands today.

The third and probably most iconic moment of this historic final were the words of English commentator Kenneth Wolstenholme when he declared, "Some people are on the pitch, they think it's all over... it is now!" His timeless words coincided with Hurst slamming the ball into the net to not only complete his hat trick but bring the curtain down on a World Cup victory that remains their only one to date (Wolstenholme, 1966).

Sports Stateside saw the Green Bay Packers win what would retroactively become known as Super Bowl I, as the NFL and the AFL officially merged as one competition. In basketball, the Boston Celtics lifted a staggering eighth championship in a row, and the Montreal Canadians took home the Stanley Cup.

Indira Gandhi broke down seemingly impenetrable barriers when she became the third Prime Minister of India—and is to date the only woman to do so. Her New Congress Party would remain in power until 1977, making her one of the most significant trailblazers in world history. Her life and achievements would see her named Woman of the Century by Time magazine in 1999.

Music saw the release of The Beach Boys' album *Pet Sounds*, The Rolling Stones' *Under My Thumb*, and the Beatles' *Revolver*. Music was changing, and albums were becoming more than just two hit singles and filler. *Pet Sounds* would inspire the Beatles to release *Sgt. Pepper,* and the Stones would try to top their English counterparts at every turn. With the emergence of bands such as The Who and The Kinks, the British Invasion was in full swing, leaving Brian Wilson to try and fight the American's corner on his own for a few massively creative years; something that would drive him into a deep, dark depression.

In Carnaby Street, London, the Swinging Sixties was in its zenith, and floral pants and brightly colored shirts were all the rage for both men and women. Flamboyant images were in, and the 'squares' were becoming something to be shunned. Although the Flower Power movement was yet to spawn from the Swinging Sixties fully, an air of superiority was descending on portions of the youth, and their need to dismiss authority and convention would trump their energy to actually do anything about it.

A sign of these easy-going, celebrity-mad times was the successful campaigning of former actor Ronald Reagan to become governor of California. Despite legitimate skepticism from some Americans and others around the world, Reagan would go on to become the 40th President of the United States—and a highly respected and fondly remembered one at that.

The kids of '66 were becoming more enthralled with the ongoing Space Race, and the toys they asked for reflected this, especially among the boys. G.I. Joe now came with astronaut gear and moon landing equipment, and the annoying robot from *Lost in Space* was one of the biggest sellers. Batman and Robin costumes proved that the superhero genre was also taking hold, and mini drum kits and electronic organs sold heavily as youngsters tried to emulate their musical heroes.

For the girls, the ever-lazy creative team at Mattel decided to just stick a plastic pony in with Barbie and her sister, Skipper. Regardless of this monotonous addition, the Barbie, Skipper, and Pony set sales went through the roof, even outselling a new batch of talking dolls that hit the shelves that Christmas.

Family board games were still hugely popular, and one that had the original name of Pretzel was released. The company that released the game, which would cause many a screaming match among siblings, had to change the name from Pretzel to Twister before bringing it out, as the former had been patented already.

In Chicago Richard Speck, mindlessly and without sane reason, murdered eight nurses in their shared residence in one night. Speck, who would garner huge media attention, showed little remorse for his actions. Ever since Bonnie and Clyde, the American public seemed to crave these sorts of news stories, and the details printed in the national press would have been watered down in any other country.

America seemed split between a need for grisly news and the peace and love that was being promoted by much of Europe; and this was never more evident than in the split opinion on their involvement in Vietnam that now ran right down the middle. The Race Riots in Atlanta added to the tension, and the Black Power movement was gaining support from all walks of life.

But '66 brought far more beautiful moments than bad. Although the riots in Atlanta were scary, they were incited for a just cause; so focusing on the results of later years rather than the property damage is a better perspective to have. Music played an inspirational part in everything that the sixties would go on to represent; and among all of the violence and sadness that occurs in the world, this decade, more than any other, fought for our right to be who we are.

# 1967: American Music Fights Back

The combined oral contraceptive pill (COCP), or simply "the pill," had been sporadically available to married women in the UK since '61. Still, even amidst a storm of religious condemnation and horrified naysayers, it was released in 1967 to every woman who wanted to decide when they were ready for pregnancy. It had been used in most of America since the beginning of the sixties, and it coincided with women's liberation and the free love vibe that was taking hold of the Western World.

Another medical breakthrough would occur that year in a hospital in Cape Town, South Africa, when a 53-year-old patient by the name of Louis Washkansky became the first patient to have a human-to-human heart transplant. Christian Barnard performed the surgery, and Washkansky—who previously had terminal heart disease—recovered to the point of being able to converse with his wife quite easily.

Unfortunately, his body reacted badly to the anti-rejection drugs in his system, and he died of pneumonia 18 days later. Barnard would attempt the surgery again a few months later on another patient. This time the patient recovered enough to be released from the hospital to return home, but died 18 months later. Despite this, advances in this type of surgery would continue to be made throughout the following years.

Britain was becoming not only the fashion and musical hub of the world, but they were blazing trails in the advancement of the nation as well. Barclays Bank unveiled the world's first successfully functioning cash dispensing machine. Back when banks opened after 10 in the morning and slammed their doors shut by three in the afternoon, getting your money out in the evening was unheard of—and you could forget about the weekends. Such a machine had been tried in the US three decades before, but it had fallen flat on its face almost instantly, and the idea was scrapped not long after, leading the States to make false claims on the patent.

In January of '67, three American astronauts tragically died in a disastrous test launch of the Apollo 1. Seen as the first crewed mission that would land on the Moon—and essentially end the Space Race—the official launch date never even arrived as a cabin fire ripped through the ship, destroying years of planning and construction. America would spend the next 18 months getting back to where they had been before the disaster.

The Beatles released what some people today still call the greatest album of all time: *Sgt. Pepper's Lonely Hearts Club Band*. Their use of string bands and experimental studio effects would change the face of music forever. In an era when most bands recorded their albums in a matter of weeks, the Beatles spent more than five months perfecting their masterpiece. Brian Wilson of The Beach Boys, whose album *Pet Sounds* had started the trend of longer recording time, apparently broke down in tears upon hearing *Peppers*.

America was starting to produce its own wave of talented musicians, and bands like The Byrds, Jefferson Airplane, and Grateful Dead showed that the British Invasion would not take over the States without a fight. This new wave of groovy music made smoking pot fashionable, and the younger generation found more ways to break free of conformity. Parents fretted over what this drug was doing to their little James and Olivia, and police started to crack down on anyone who looked even slightly high.

In cinema, *The Graduate* was released. This movie skyrocketed the career of a young Dustin Hoffman, and gave the world the character of Mrs. Robinson. This would change the lives of millions of teenage boys around the globe, as they finally discovered that they were, in fact, not odd at all for fancying their best friend's mother. Other big hits included the biopic *Bonnie and Clyde,* and the Paul Newman classic *Cool Hand Luke.*

Glasgow Celtic became the first-ever British team to lift the European Cup, beating the mighty Inter Milan 2-1 in the final at the Estadio Nacional, near Lisbon, Portugal. Inter, who had taken the lead early, instantly resorted to their famous "11 man defense" after the goal. The Lisbon Lions battered them for the rest of the match, and Bobby Murdoch's deflected effort with five minutes left proved to be the winner. One of the most astonishing facts about that night was that all but two of Celtic's team were born within ten miles of their home stadium, Celtic Park.

Matt Busby's Manchester United team lifted the league title in England, while Spurs took the FA Cup home. Billie Jean King won her second of many Wimbledon titles in tennis, a sport that she would go on to dominate in the coming years. She would also become an extremely important figure in the ongoing battle for women's rights.

St. Louis won the World Series, taking out the favored Boston Red Sox, while Toronto lifted the Stanley Cup. In basketball, the Philadelphia 76ers beat the San

Francisco Warriors to lift the NBA Championship, in what would be the first final in 11 years not to feature the Boston Celtics.

The cities of America became a hotbed for rioting and looting as racial tensions continued to boil over. Martin Luther King Jr's calls for peaceful protests in the preceding years seemed to be falling on deaf ears, and amidst the war that still raged in Vietnam, the people of America became divided yet again. It was starting to look like the good vibes being sent out by the rest of the world were having little or no effect on a country that portrayed itself as the greatest on the planet.

Throughout it all, however, positive steps were being taken. Thurgood Marshall became the first African American in history to be Associate Justice of the Supreme Court of America, a position he would hold until 1991. Marshall, who had originally been appointed to the Court of Appeals by the progressive John F. Kennedy went on to earn an endless number of honors throughout his life *and* after his death. Many colleges and law schools have since named their buildings and libraries after the great man.

Twiggy, an English model who epitomized the Swinging Sixties, was to be seen swanning up and down catwalks the world over, and her appearances at every trendy hotspot became the stuff of legends. Her image would become an integral part of sixties pop culture, and she somehow managed to squeeze an acting and musical career in between it all.

Corgi toy cars became popular, but their intricate design and high prices meant that only a lucky few could realistically afford them. Possibly every kid in the Western World owned at least one Matchbox car, though, with the company producing millions of the less detailed but more affordable toy cars. The Aurora Auto Racing set in America and Scaletrix in Europe were the most sought-after toys in '67. Although they were extremely expensive, many siblings asked their parents if they could lump all of their presents together that Christmas and share the electric car racing game. Most were disappointed!

For the girls, proof that women's rights still had a long way to go was confirmed when the Little Girl Loves to Clean set came out. Equipped with a mini brush, dustpan, apron, and an array of other cleaning utensils, it seemed that the toy companies were hell-bent on refusing to face the fact that times were meant to be a'changing. Other toys for the ladies included a stuffed Lassie teddy and the slightly less sexist Little Girl Loves a Tea Party set.

With the acceptance of the pill in the UK, and it's already having been sold in most other countries around the world, it seemed that progressive steps were being made. But with toys such as Little Girl Loves to Clean still presumed acceptable, it was also painfully obvious that there was still a long way to go. All of this could be said for racial inequality, too, as the riots throughout America illustrated.

But on the whole, peace and love still continued to spread the good vibes it had set out to; and the younger generation was continuing to raise their voice higher. Unlike the decades before the sixties, it seemed that some of it was getting through. Music and television were having more of an impact; and unlike today, the things that the musicians and movies had to say were nearly all positive. The sixties were in full flow in '67, and the groovy vibe that it is famed for today was continuing to shake the old ideals to their core.

# 1968: Assassinations and Vietnam

America dominated the news in a year that seemed dedicated to the carnage ripping the country in half, never more epitomized than by the assassination of Dr. Martin Luther King Jr on April 4. King, who had just given a sermon in Memphis where he delivered his now fabled "I have been to the Promised Land" speech, was shot later that evening as he stood on his hotel balcony, by a man named James Earl Ray.

The killer, whose rifle and binoculars were found near the crime scene, would plead guilty on the advice of his lawyer in hope of avoiding the electric chair. Upon being informed later that the death penalty would not have been an option, Ray fired his lawyer and claimed that he had not actually pulled the trigger. His new defense angle of claiming a conspiracy was ignored, and he was sentenced to 99 years in jail.

In Vietnam, the Tet Offensive was launched by the North Vietnamese and the Viet Cong, with a surprise attack against Hue, Saigon, and other major areas in South Vietnam. The horrors of what occurred were beamed back to over 58 million American homes, and the images would prove to be the proverbial straw that broke the camel's back, so far as the public was concerned. Now, not only were the youth of America appalled at their involvement in the war, but the older generation were too. With the anger toward America that was boiling over in Europe and the rest of the world, Lyndon Johnson and his advisors now knew that they were no longer backed by the majority.

With an election on the horizon, the peoples' golden child, Robert F. Kennedy, agreed to run against the war-loving Johnson. Kennedy had refused to enter the race in the preceding years. Now, realizing he not only had the support of the public but that his older brother's hard work was being undone, he decided that it was his duty to step in and help his country.

In a dark, ironic twist, Kennedy announced his plan to run on the same day that American troops slaughtered over 500 innocent Vietnamese civilians, in what would become known as the My Lai Massacre. RFK would not have known about this at the time, but from our present-day vantage point it can be used as a marker to show just how needed young Bobby was. Things in Vietnam were getting out of control, and a change was needed as soon as possible.

In Britain, the announcement that "the pill" would become widely available—which caused public outcry—was quickly followed up by another bill being passed that legalized abortion. In an argument that still rages today (and probably always will), the two sides dug in their heels and refused to be swayed in either direction. With both views being so passionately shouted from either corner, any chance of them agreeing on even the smallest detail was impossible. Although the bill was passed, women who sought abortions were shunned and humiliated in many towns and villages.

Enoch Powell, the British politician, gave his famous "Rivers of Blood" speech to a group of Conservatives at a hotel in Birmingham. Powell, who was a child genius and considered to be one of the most eloquent men alive at the time, raged at the ongoing influx of immigrants landing on British soil. Although his speech was meant to build up some resistance to this, it actually backfired and, over time, became a focal point for people to sit down and discuss the matter rationally. Thankfully, the speech would mean that his political career would never again carry as much weight as it once had.

It all went on to show that racial inequality was still heavily present in politics and in the world as a whole, but the protests of the youth in the early sixties were becoming a lot bigger and more effective. Students everywhere were taking to the streets to protest any number of things, from the aforementioned racial equality to the lack of financial support for student fees.

Following the news of the slaughtering of innocent Vietnamese civilians in Vietnam and the assassination of Dr. Martin Luther King Jr, rioting in America grew out of control. Hundreds of homes and businesses all over the country became nothing more than broken glass and ash, and the youth of Europe joined them in their stance. Student protests took place in Britain, West Germany, Poland, and Paris. The latter became known as Bloody Monday, as police forces stormed the crowds with weapons, leaving hundreds of French youths hospitalized.

With the news of unrest spreading, the French workers stood by their younger counterparts in a move that would force then President of France, Charles de Gaulle, to announce immediate elections and threaten military action.

Despite all of the protests, sports across Britain and Europe had never been so popular—especially in England, as Manchester United's Busby Babes lifted the European Cup for the first time. This would not only be the first time for the Red Devils, but for any English club. To make matters even more astounding, Sir Matt Busby managed to achieve this after the club had lost seven of its first-team players less than a decade before, in the Munich Air Disaster.

United's neighbors, Manchester City, lifted the English league trophy while Liverpool took home the FA Cup. Stateside, the Green Bay Packers won Super Bowl II, and one OJ Simpson was the overwhelming winner of the Heisman Trophy that year. The honor of NBA champions went to the Boston Celtics, who reclaimed the throne after their brief fall from grace the previo— us year. In baseball, the Detroit Tigers took home the World Series.

The Beatles recorded together for the last time, in a studio in Twickenham, London, where they were filmed rehearsing the timeless hit, "Hey Jude." The song, written by McCartney for John Lennon's son Julian, whose parents were going through a divorce, would be widely regarded as the zenith of musical collaboration; and everything came together to create what many would call the greatest song ever written. Amazingly, the double album released by the band later that year—*The White Album*—would somehow not find a place for "Hey Jude," despite having 30 tracks on it.

In December, the Space Race took a huge turn when the United States leapfrogged their Soviet enemies by becoming the first nation to orbit the moon in a crewed spacecraft, Apollo 8, and bring it back down to Earth safely. It was seen as a milestone, especially given the horrors of the failed test launch of Apollo 1 the previous year—yet nobody could have predicted just how soon a man would walk on the surface of it.

The tensions in America became the stuff of a Hollywood tale when yet another assassination rocked the country. Robert F. Kennedy, who had just finished giving an address at the Ambassador Hotel in Los Angeles after winning the Democratic Presidential poll, was gunned down by Sirhan Sirhan. Upon questioning, the Jordanian shooter would claim that he was angry at RFK's perceived support of Israel during the Six Day War. Robert's death would open up the presidential race for Richard Nixon, who seemed to slip in the back door while the public had their back turned.

All of the bloodshed in the States left the country living in fear, and as cities burned and politicians fell, it was becoming clear that America was in a pretty bad place. All of this caused the music scene to explode, as people needed an escape from the endless streams of horrific news that seemed to have become part of daily life; and they found it in the passion coming out of their speakers.

Europe tried to have an opinion on what was happening in the States, and students continued to protest in the colleges and schools. But the American leaders were stubborn, and the bombs continued to fall on Vietnam regardless of public outcry. The peace and love carried into the decade by the younger generation looked to be getting trampled under the boots of power-hungry politicians; but the youth still refused to back down.

# 1969: One Giant Leap For Mankind

If '68 was a year of turmoil and tension, '69 saw an explosion of breakthroughs, timeless moments, and feel-good events—none more so than when Neil Armstrong planted his foot on the Moon for the very first time. The Space Race was effectively over; and the Americans, who had played catch up from the first moment, had now completed one of the human race's greatest achievements.

The words, "That's one small step for man, one giant leap for mankind," would forever be etched into the minds of those who watched it live. Buzz Aldrin would step down onto the Moon's surface soon after, and upon safely returning to Earth, the three astronauts aboard the Apollo 11 would become celebrities of unprecedented magnitude (Armstrong, 1969).

Space-themed toys, movies, and TV shows grew in demand, and the exploits of the Americans to achieve such a miracle seemed to be the very thing that calmed the tensions that had been rocking the nation. Whether this was actually a factor can never be proven, but it seemed that such a monumental event somehow showed the people of the world just how small they were in the grand scheme of things. How could we fight amongst ourselves when we were not only such amazingly creative beings, but had so much left to achieve together?

Technological advances boomed, and in a short space of time to follow, they would reach speeds of change that even the most ridiculous Sci-Fi movie at the time could not have predicted. Along with humans walking on the Moon, the Advanced Research Projects Agency Network (ARPANET) successfully sent a message from one computer to another. As insignificant as sending one word might seem today, this technological breakthrough was the birth of our most influential creation to date: the Internet.

The effect of this discovery—which was, understandably, buried beneath the news coverage of the Moon Landing—would make unsurmountable changes to our lives today. However, the full effects wouldn't be seen until the nineties. Along with satellite TV, which was really taking off in the States, the way we sent and received information was becoming quicker and more instantaneous than it had ever been. Travel was moving in the same direction, and the *Boeing 747* made its maiden flight from Paris in the same year.

The shows being broadcast in '69 remained Western-themed, with *Bonanza* and *Gunsmoke* still topping the viewing charts. But they were losing their grip, and sitcoms and chat shows would soon be the flavor of the seventies. Of course, Sci-Fi was continuing its resurgence, thanks to Neil Armstrong and his crew.

A little show called *Sesame Street* aired for the first time that year. Television companies such as NBC and CBS were starting to realize that children's TV was a way to make a whole lot of money. Now, not only could they sign huge advertising deals with the toy companies, but the image of a screaming kid stomping their feet and getting exactly what they wanted was creeping into American life. If the kids were running things at home, they would also choose what the family watched on the box.

The BBC debuted their first all-color format in Britain; but unlike their cousins across the Atlantic, British shows were hitting a golden age of comedy and drama. Monty Python shocked the world with its bizarre yet genius outlook on comedy, and began to rip up the rule book in '69 when the first episode of *Monty Python's Flying Circus* aired on BBC.

Other styles of comedy that you didn't have to think about were also popular. Benny Hill head-slapped his way into the nation's heart with his more on-the-nose style of humor. Morcombe and Wise debuted the second season of their classic show, proving that this new love for comedy in Britain and Ireland was far from a flash in the pan. While hit American programs like *Star Trek* were being broadcast alongside all of the original British creations.

Along with the progressive attitude that was taking hold of Britain concerning abortion and women's rights, they also took another step forward with the abolition of the death penalty. Although many would disagree with this ruling, most believed it to be outdated and inhumane. It was another tick of a box for a nation that seemed to be paving the way for the rest to follow.

In music, two live events—drastically different in attendance—left a deep footprint in the history of music. The first, in January of '69, saw the Beatles perform an impromptu gig on top of their Apple Corps headquarters in Saville Row, London. The 42-minute set was a sort of rehearsal for their new material; and the band, who had refused to play in public for years, knocked out nine takes of five new songs to the unsuspecting crowd of mostly office workers on their lunch break. After the band ended with a timeless rendition of "Get Back," John Lennon signed off with the words, "I'd like to say thank you on behalf of the group and ourselves, and I hope we passed the audition" (Lennon, 1969).

The band would also release their final album together in September before they split. Tensions had been running high for a while among the four members, and rumors were rife that the breakup was imminent. Paul McCartney managed to convince the rest to go into the studio one last time to show the world what they could do, and the album that came out—along with the iconic cover—would forever be known as a work of art. *Abbey Road* was a masterpiece, and it was seen as the perfect way for the most influential band of all time to part ways.

The other event that possibly created more iconic music moments than any other was Woodstock. The concert, held in a dairy farm in New York was billed as "Three Days of Peace and Music," and the scenes that would be captured on camera would prove this to be the case. Some of the bands and musicians to play there included Jimi Hendrix, The Who, Jefferson Airplane, Janis Joplin, Santana, The Band, Grateful Dead, Joe Cocker, and many more. The Beatles would miss out; yet the lineup still threw together a group of talent in one place that was unparalleled and will forever remain that way.

American sports were more popular than ever, and now with the events being beamed into nearly every home each day, the public could keep a much closer eye on their favorite teams. Super Bowl III was won by the New York Jets in a pulsating match against the Baltimore Colts. A terrible sporting year for Baltimore (and a great one for New York) was rounded off as the Baltimore Orioles lost to the New York Mets, completing a double for New Yorkers to celebrate. Amazingly, the Boston Celtics defended the NBA championship yet again.

Boxing lost a legend of the sport when Rocky Marciano died one day shy of his 46th birthday, when the *Cessna*

*172* he was on crashed due to bad weather and an inexperienced pilot. The Brockton Blockbuster remains the only world heavyweight champion to go undefeated throughout his whole career, winning all 49 of his fights.

In England, Leeds United won the English league title for the first time in their history, finishing six points above Liverpool. The FA Cup was lifted by Manchester City once more. At the same time, Newcastle United won their only ever European trophy when they took home the Inter-Cities Fairs Cup (modern-day Europa League).

In fashion, military jackets and war memorabilia were being worn ironically by the youth as the revolution continued to pulse amidst the soundtrack of the war in Vietnam. It would be four years before America withdrew her troops, but one can only imagine how long their occupation there would have lasted if it weren't for the outcry of the youth of the sixties generation.

After the slump of '68, the year 1969 was the tonic that the world needed. Dreaming big was the order of the day, and this was typified by the revolutionary and groundbreaking music that was carrying the people into the seventies. People were ready for a change, and what had begun with an impossible dream of walking on the Moon in 1960 ended with humans achieving that very thing nine years later. It was now okay to allow yourself to imagine; and the younger generation, who made the sixties the most iconic decade in history, had shown this to the world through their vision of peace and love.

*****

What more can we say about the sixties than, wow. A decade that saw so many changes will always be remembered fondly. Sure, some of them were negative and even devastating; but as far as profound changes go, there probably isn't a ten-year period that comes close.

Even setting aside the Space Race and the massive growth of television, the changes that have had just as much of a lasting effect have been the morals and decency that the sixties tried to promote. With the shift in music and cinema, the world stepped up its game creatively. The doors that had been opened by the sixties would be gratefully entered into by many more artistic men and women when the seventies rolled around.

Many more battles would need to be fought, both for freedom and for power, but the wheels of revolution had been set in motion and soon even the voting age would be dropped. All of this proved that the protests, music, and endless campaigning of the youth really had been heard. This is why the sixties is remembered with such passion and gratitude among the people today.

When we think back over the decade, our minds are drawn to so many of the amazing events we've covered here. It's impossible to land on just one, as each time we try we have to stop ourselves and say, "Oh, but what about the time…"

Living through the sixties and being able to reminisce must be a wonderful gift; but for those of us who didn't, we can only pay homage to it by learning as much as we can about a time when love was free, and the Moon came into reach. Remember to dream big—because if the Swinging Sixties taught us anything, it's that nothing is impossible if you really want it!

# References

BBC Sport. (2014, June 10). World Cup moments: "They think it's all over..." *BBC Sport*. https://www.bbc.com/sport/av/football/27005797

Burnton, S. (2018, March 22). "World Cup stunning moments: The Battle of Santiago | Simon Burnton." *The Guardian*. https://www.theguardian.com/football/blog/2014/mar/04/stunning-moments-no4-battle-of-santiago

History.com Editors. (2019, January 30). "The 1969 Moon Landing. HISTORY; A&E." *Television Networks*. https://www.history.com/topics/space-exploration/moon-landing-1969

James, J. (2021, January 30). "Unassuming London rooftop for The Beatles last show 52 years ago." *MyLondon*. https://www.mylondon.news/news/nostalgia/unassuming-london-rooftop-played-host-19734624

**Images:** All images sourced from Pixabay.

Printed in Great Britain
by Amazon